BENJAMIN
BRITTEN

A LIFE OF MUSIC

Front cover: Publicity photograph
of Benjamin Britten dated 1968.

Back cover: Snape Maltings concert hall,
Suffolk (author's photograph).

BENJAMIN
BRITTEN

A LIFE OF MUSIC

TIMOTHY GILBERT

BREWIN BOOKS

BREWIN BOOKS
19 Enfield Ind. Estate,
Redditch,
Worcestershire,
B97 6BY
www.brewinbooks.com

Published by Brewin Books 2025

A CIP catalogue record for this book is
available from the British Library.

ISBN: 978-1-85858-778-3

Printed and bound in Great Britain
by Halstan & Co. Ltd.

Contents

Benjamin Britten, 1913-1976.

Introduction

I remember hearing the news of Benjamin Britten's death; the solitary walk along a canal towpath that I took to mark the sad, if not unanticipated, event. Instinctively I turned to a recording of the *Four Sea Interludes* from his opera *Peter Grimes*, performed by Eduard van Beinum – a champion of the composer (and a much-loved music director) – and the wonderful Amsterdam Concertgebouw Orchestra.

I had discovered Ben's music a decade earlier, in the mid-1960s. These were times when, taking refuge from the harsh realities of a Black Country grammar school, I tuned in to The Third Programme and its successor Radio Three. I owe to these channels during their halcyon days – that is, before the relentless quest for 'new audiences' and 'inclusion' took hold – a huge debt of gratitude. Another early discovery, I might add, was the music of Edmund Rubbra, to this day the most shamefully neglected of all significant English composers.

To anyone wishing to discover more about Britten and Aldeburgh, I would simply say: read Ronald Blythe's *The Time by the Sea*. Here they will find Ben, Peter, Imo (Imogen Holst), Morgan (the writer E.M. Forster), and many others besides.

In the decades since his death Britten's music has never – perhaps unusually – suffered even a temporary eclipse. The music and the man who created it continue to exercise fascination to new generations of performers and listeners. I hope that this slender volume may encourage readers to explore for themselves why this may be so. I am particularly grateful to David Matthews for the interest he has shown in this project, and for his helpful comments. Luigi rendered invaluable technical assistance. Brewin Books were, once again, exemplary in their support. Any errors are solely the author's responsibility.

It is not for me to offer any assessment of Britten's stature as a composer; for such a task I am wholly unqualified. We do, however, have on record the judgement of his colleague and friend Michael Tippett: '… Britten has been for me the most purely musical person I have ever met and have ever known.' His recorded legacy, especially live performances caught 'on the wing' as it were, provides compelling vindication of the truth of this statement.

The text falls into three sections: a biographical outline; a view of Britten's personality and relationships with friends and colleagues; and an impression of the recorded legacy, both Britten's and other composers' music.

I dedicate this book with admiration and affection to George Vass.

Autumn 2024

1.

Biographical outline

B enjamin Britten was born in Lowestoft, Suffolk, on 22 November 1913. Appropriately this is also the feast day of St Cecilia, patron saint of music. Britten's father was a dental surgeon and his mother, who had a fine soprano voice, was honorary secretary of Lowestoft Choral Society. The family home faced the North Sea. That sea, its changing moods perfectly captured in his music, always meant a great deal to him.

Britten's family – he was the youngest of four children – enjoyed making music. His father did not want a wireless or gramophone in the house for fear of discouraging people from making music for themselves. Benjamin received his earliest piano lessons from his mother and he was no older than five when he made his first attempts at composition; he was endlessly fascinated by the dots and patterns that the music made all over the page. He wrote literally reams of music during his boyhood, some of which he later arranged for strings and published under the title *Simple Symphony* (1934). At the age of ten he began to study harmony, by which time he was also learning the viola.

His parents recognised their son's remarkable musical gift and, through his viola teacher, Audrey Alston, he was able to meet the composer Frank Bridge at the Norwich Triennial Festival in 1927. Three years earlier he had been 'knocked sideways' on hearing Bridge conduct a performance of his orchestral suite *The Sea*. He now began composition lessons with Bridge during the school holidays. Learning from the older man's example, Britten became meticulous about marking every detail on his scores. There were also, at Bridge's suggestion, piano lessons from Harold Samuel in London.

This intensive musical training, however, did not involve the neglect of his general education. From a local preparatory school he proceeded to Gresham's School, Holt, in Norfolk, where a feature was the chamber music recitals given by members of staff and senior pupils. In July 1930 he left school, having won an open scholarship in composition to the Royal College of Music in London.

At the college Britten studied the piano with Arthur Benjamin and composition with John Ireland ('*terribly* critical and enough to take the heart out of any one!'), but he was not able to deepen his understanding of contemporary music to the extent that he fervently wished, and often felt frustrated. By way of compensation he attended, often in the company of the Bridges, several first performances of new works at the Queen's Hall. Much of his time was spent practising and composing in his attic room in the private boarding house where he lodged.

The set of choral variations, *A Boy was Born*, composed early in 1933, already showed his distinctive response to poetry and his technical assurance but, remarkably, among his early works, only the *Sinfonietta* (Opus 1) for ten instruments was performed at the college during his student days. It was through the Macnaghten-Lemare concerts of new music, given at the Ballet Club Theatre, that Benjamin Britten's name came to the notice of a wider public.

In his final year he was awarded a scholarship for study and travel abroad. He had hoped to study with Alban Berg in Vienna, but his parents were advised that such an influence might not be helpful. Instead he had to fall back on his own musical resources to chart his own course.

Britten left the Royal College of Music in 1933. Still only nineteen, he was determined to earn his living through composition. In this sense, an invitation from John Grierson, director of the GPO Film Unit, to work on documentary films was just what he needed. More than that, the discipline imposed by limited resources, a tight schedule, and the actual working conditions of the unit, provided him with a fund of experience. With Britten, such necessary restrictions were invariably a spur rather than a hindrance to creativity. In 1936 he wrote the music for two classic documentaries, *Coal Face* and *Night Mail*, working alongside the poet W.H. Auden, who was employed by the unit as a scriptwriter. Composing simply for a group of instruments, he produced a whole series of economical and realistic scores, depicting a wide variety of everyday sounds. As the unit's resident composer, he was already working as a useful member of the community. Besides his work in the film studio Britten became aware, largely through his friendship with Auden, of the exciting possibilities offered by the theatre and radio, and his incidental music made an important contribution to the development of these media during the late 1930s.

Britten collaborated extensively with Auden during the pre-war period. An important commission in 1936 from the Norfolk and Norwich Festival gave rise to his first song cycle, *Our Hunting Fathers*, a brilliant setting for high voice and orchestra of a somewhat satirical text, devised by Auden, with a theme of man's relations with animals and written in the context of the worsening political situation in Europe. Britten dedicated it to the music publisher Ralph Hawkes, with whom he had recently signed a contract.

Composer and poet alike viewed with alarm the apparently relentless advance of fascism and the malaise that was affecting Europe. *Ballad of Heroes*, with words by Auden and Randall Swingler, was composed as a memorial to the men of the British Battalion of the International Brigade who had lost their lives in Spain. Other pieces, the unison song *Pacifist March*, written for the Peace Pledge Union, and an unaccompanied chorus *Advance Democracy*, show his preoccupations. *Variations on a Theme of Frank Bridge* for string orchestra, which was far more significant as a purely musical statement, belongs to the same period. First performed by the Boyd Neel Orchestra at the 1937 Salzburg Festival, this dazzling and inventive score established Britten almost overnight as a composer of international stature and it remains a landmark among works of its genre.

In the late spring of 1939 Britten left for America. Like Auden, who had already settled there, he felt that he might be able to develop more freely as an artist away from the constraints of the Old World. The prospect for Europe was scarcely reassuring. He was accompanied by his companion the tenor Peter Pears, who had been a member of the BBC Singers for two years and had already toured America with the New English Singers. Looking back many years later, he remembered himself as 'a discouraged young composer – muddled, fed-up and looking for work, longing to be used.'

On their arrival, Britten and Pears travelled first to Canada but they soon settled in Amityville, Long Island, in the company of the remarkable and generous Mayer family. They gave a number of recitals and Britten also made his mark as soloist in his own Piano Concerto, which he had premièred at a Promenade Concert in 1938. Like the Violin Concerto, one of the first fruits of his American period and a deeper, more introspective work, it revealed a preoccupation, even when writing for full symphony orchestra, with matters of textural clarity. Britten's style was maturing rapidly. The song cycles

Les Illuminations (the poems by Rimbaud) and the *Seven Sonnets of Michelangelo* showed his instinctive way with words and music, an almost uncanny ability to set poetry, and not only English poetry, to music. The Michelangelo cycle, composed in October 1940, was the first work written specifically with Pears's vocal qualities in mind. The operetta *Paul Bunyan*, based on the folk legend of the giant pioneer lumberjack, was his biggest single collaboration with Auden and another important first venture. Though withdrawn after a short, unsuccessful run at Columbia University, New York, in May 1941, it showed how keen Britten's theatrical sense already was.

There was a time when Britten seriously considered settling in the United States and becoming, like Auden, an American citizen. But gradually he came to understand that, as a composer, he needed roots. His roots were in England, in Suffolk. The strain of separation made him physically ill and for several months he was unable to work. During a stay in California he came across a copy of *The Listener*, which included an article by E.M. Forster about the Suffolk poet George Crabbe. The nagging conviction that he must return home now became irresistible.

During the long months of waiting for a passage he heard a performance of his orchestral *Sinfonia da Requiem*, given in Boston under Serge Koussevitzky. The conductor, sensing the work's dramatic power, asked pointedly why he had not written a full-scale opera. Britten replied that before he could commit himself to so large an undertaking he would need a degree of security from financial pressures. He had by this time read Crabbe's poem *The Borough*, and within it the story of Peter Grimes. The idea of turning it into an opera seemed to have definite possibilities. Hearing of this, Koussevitzky made arrangements for Britten to receive a grant of $1,000 from the Koussevitzky Music Foundation, which would enable him at least to start work on the opera.

Britten arrived in England in April 1942, having made the hazardous crossing in a small Swedish cargo boat, at the end of a long convoy. While at sea he composed the *Hymn to St Cecilia* (the text by Auden) for unaccompanied chorus, and *A Ceremony of Carols*, settings of old English poems for treble voices and harp.

Returning to a country at war both he and Peter Pears appeared before a tribunal for conscientious objectors, which exempted them from military service. They subsequently gave a series of recitals under the auspices of CEMA (the Council for the Encouragement of Music and the Arts), and in the summer of 1945 Britten joined with Yehudi Menuhin to give concerts for the Allied troops in Europe, also visiting German concentration camps.

It was many months, however, before Britten was able to devote all his energies to the opera. There were concerts to be given and other compositions that absorbed his attention, notably the festival cantata *Rejoice in the Lamb*, and the *Serenade* for tenor, horn and strings, an evocative setting of his own selection of diverse poems with the common theme of evening.

Britten worked at his opera *Peter Grimes* throughout 1944. His home at this time was a converted windmill in the village of Snape, a few miles from Aldeburgh, which he had bought in 1937. Largely through the faith and enthusiasm of Joan Cross, the director of the Sadler's Wells company, it was with *Peter Grimes* that their theatre reopened on 7 June 1945, exactly a month after the end of the war in Europe. Peter Pears sang the title role and Joan Cross that of his friend, the village schoolmistress Ellen Orford. From the very first night the opera was an overwhelming success. The characterisation of the individual townsfolk, as drawn by Britten and his librettist Montagu Slater, is marvellously acute and vivid. In his treatment of the fisherman Grimes, a solitary figure hounded by the community to which he does not conform, Britten revealed a great quality of compassion, which in the next few years was to strike a responsive chord in the hearts of audiences the world over. The restless sea, magnificently depicted in the orchestral interludes, is the unchanging background of the drama. Here, at last, was an English opera of international stature; truly a new era was beginning.

In the post-Grimes period, Britten showed himself to be a remarkably prolific and assured composer. From his student days he had felt a special affinity with the music of Henry Purcell, the composer of *Dido and Aeneas*. The 250th anniversary of Purcell's death fell in November 1945 and Britten commemorated it with his settings of *The Holy Sonnets of John Donne*, a work born out of the harrowing circumstances of his recent German visit, and his String Quartet No.2 which has – in homage to Purcell – a chacony as its finale. His central concern, however, lay in the development of a truly native opera. In the immediate aftermath of war, with austerity the keynote, it would be unrealistic to expect much of the established London houses. Here, as elsewhere (his reaction to the Maltings fire a case in point), he was always immensely practical.

The pressing need was for an opera group of chamber proportions, who were able to mount productions of new works at non-excessive cost, and then take them on tour. Chamber opera could be staged in comparatively modest provincial theatres, thereby reaching out to a much wider audience. These ideas led to the formation of the Glyndebourne English Opera Company, which was reconstituted in 1947 as the English Opera Group. The opera that Britten wrote for them, *The Rape of Lucretia*, first heard at Glyndebourne in July 1946, and performed no fewer than eighty times in its first season, required only eight singers and a chamber orchestra of twelve players. The following year saw the première of the comedy *Albert Herring*, another chamber opera though a far remove from the classical tragedy of 'Lucretia'. The plot, based on a short story by Maupassant, was given a local setting in an East Suffolk market town. In the summer of 1947, shortly after the opera's first performance, Britten moved out of his mill at Snape and bought a house in Aldeburgh that overlooked the sea.

Despite this promising start, the cost of taking even chamber operas on tour proved to be prohibitive, so the composer and his associates began to make plans to hold their own festival, albeit of modest proportions: 'a few concerts given by friends', as Peter Pears put it. The first Aldeburgh Festival opened on 5 June 1948 with the first performance in the parish church of Britten's cantata *Saint Nicolas*. The next year his new work was an opera for children, *The Little Sweep*, or *Let's make an Opera*, which was staged in the Jubilee Hall. In both there were opportunities for the audience to join in.

The festival was never envisaged as an exclusively musical event, but has always been distinguished by its local character. In 1948 there were exhibitions of East Anglian paintings and models of the designs for *Peter Grimes* were on display in the Moot Hall. Exhibitions and lectures taking in a range of the arts have always been a feature. Britten himself often took to the stage as a piano accompanist or to play duets with such artists as Sviatoslav Richter and, through his advocacy, comparatively neglected figures – his teacher Frank Bridge and Percy Grainger, to name but two – began to receive their due acclaim.

Many of Britten's compositions were inspired by the artistry of individual performers: friends who regularly returned to Aldeburgh to make music and give pleasure. The *Six Metamorphoses after Ovid* for unaccompanied oboe, which he wrote in 1951 for Joy Boughton to play on the water at Thorpeness, is a delightful case in point. Among other works of his middle years, *Canticle II, Abraham and Isaac* (the text from the Chester Miracle Play), for alto, tenor and piano, was composed as a tribute to the vocal talents of Kathleen Ferrier and Peter Pears; while its successor, *Still falls the Rain,* first performed in January 1955 at the Wigmore Hall, found Britten again at the piano, this time with Pears and the horn player Dennis Brain.

In 1967, with the conversion of the old maltings at Snape, the festival acquired a splendid concert hall. Tragically, only two years later, it was gutted by fire after the opening night at the Jubilee Hall and the programme had to be completely reorganised. Through great determination, the rebuilding of The Maltings was completed in time for the 1970 festival, the acoustics perhaps even finer than before.

Britten's belief in the future of English opera as a vital force is reflected in his realisations of other composers' works. His arrangement of John Gay's ever-popular *The Beggar's Opera* was first heard at the Arts Theatre in Cambridge in 1948. Besides encouraging contemporary opera, it was also part of the brief of the English Opera

Group to mount productions of classical works, and three years later he joined with Imogen Holst to produce a performing edition of Purcell's *Dido and Aeneas*. Another compliment to his great predecessor was paid in *The Young Person's Guide to the Orchestra*, a set of thirteen variations based on one of Purcell's hornpipes, with a culminating fugue. The score was originally intended to accompany an educational film, illustrating the instruments of the orchestra; Britten was able to draw upon his wealth of experience as a composer of documentary music.

For his next opera Britten returned to the sea and to a larger canvas. *Billy Budd*, the libretto adapted by E.M. Forster and Eric Crozier from Herman Melville's story, was commissioned by the Arts Council as a contribution to the Festival of Britain in 1951. The entire action is set on board *HMS Indomitable* in the period of the French revolutionary wars and centres on the fate of Billy Budd, an impressed recruit, who is destroyed by the malevolence of the ship's master-at-arms, John Claggart. There is within the opera a sense of an overwhelming conflict between the forces of good, personified in Billy, and evil. The omnipresent sea and an exclusively male cast add to the unremitting intensity of the drama.

The following opera, *Gloriana*, composed by Britten to mark the coronation of Queen Elizabeth II, was initially much less favourably received. Far from being a celebration of a vanished golden age, the libretto draws on the character of Elizabeth I, the ageing queen, in some detail. At its core is her relationship with the much younger Earl of Essex.

In the autumn of 1953 Britten set to work on a new opera, which this time was conceived for the chamber medium. *The Turn of the Screw* to a libretto based on Henry James's compelling story, was commissioned for the Venice Biennale Festival of 1954. With an Essex country house as the outwardly tranquil setting, two ghosts struggle to take possession of the souls of Miles and Flora, young orphan siblings. Their sinister, corrupting influence is countered by the children's new governess but in the end she cannot save Miles. The opera takes the form of sixteen short scenes, which are linked by a set of instrumental variations on a twelve-note theme.

During the winter of 1955-1956 Britten and Pears went on a memorable tour, beginning in Europe and taking in Bali, Japan and India. Some of Britten's music for the ballet *The Prince of the Pagodas* was inspired by the Balinese gamelan, whilst in Tokyo he saw a performance of a traditional Japanese Noh play, which made a deep and abiding impression. Almost a decade later he drew upon the whole experience of this visit in composing *Curlew River*, the first of his church parables.

Towards the end of 1957 Britten moved to the Red House, a rambling property just out of Aldeburgh, which was to be his home for the rest of his life. During this time he was working on *Noye's Fludde*, a children's opera set to a libretto again taken from the Chester Miracle Plays. As in *Saint Nicolas* there are hymns for the audience to sing, although in the later work they are far more effectively part of the dramatic structure. *Noye's Fludde* found a perfect setting in the nearby medieval church at Orford, where it was first performed during the 1958 Aldeburgh Festival by a large body of young singers and players from East Suffolk, who were supplemented by a small group of professional instrumentalists.

The renovation and enlargement of the Jubilee Hall, carried out the following year, opened up possibilities for a new full-length opera from Britten in time for the 1960 Festival. With Peter Pears, he decided to prepare a libretto based on Shakespeare's *A Midsummer Night's Dream* and, although this involved severely abridging the text, only one line of the original was altered.

As a practical composer, very conscious of his obligations as a member of society, Britten undertook a number of important commissions. What comes over, time and again, is the sheer professionalism and flair that he brought to the task. Often the impulse was broadly humanitarian, as with the *Cantata Misericordium*, commissioned for the centenary of the Red Cross in 1963, or, on a smaller scale, the anthem *Voices for Today*, which he wrote for the twentieth anniversary of the United Nations. Whatever the nature or size of the occasion, Britten's response was never merely routine. He once remarked, "... almost every piece I have ever written has been composed with a certain occasion in mind, and usually for definite performers, and certainly always *human* ones".

The commission that gave rise to the *War Requiem* prompted one of his most imaginative large-scale works, one that enabled him to give full expression to his lifelong pacifist convictions. The occasion was the consecration in May 1962 of the new Coventry Cathedral, a symbol of hope in a divided world. Britten had the inspired idea of combining the text of the Latin Mass for the Dead with a group of poems by the young Wilfred Owen, who was himself killed only days before the Armistice in 1918. The words of the Mass are set for soprano soloist, chorus and full orchestra, while in the foreground are the two male soloists (soldiers in the heat of battle, as experienced by Owen himself) and the chamber orchestra. Poet and composer shared a common outrage that an ostensibly Christian society could come to view human life as something expendable, trivial even. Britten's choice of soloists – a Russian soprano, a British tenor and a German baritone – underlines that spirit of reconciliation enshrined in the Cathedral itself and so movingly achieved in the closing pages of his work. As for Britten's own beliefs, they were always humanitarian, never dogmatically Christian. He once remarked that he liked to think of himself as a Christian in his music.

The *War Requiem* and its implicit message brought Britten's name before a wider public than ever before. Looking back, it can also be seen as a watershed moment in his creative development, for in the following years his style, as distinctive as ever, acquired new qualities of reticence and austerity. During the 1960s his dramatic gifts found expression chiefly through his highly original conception of the parable for church performance. Between 1964 and 1968, working in collaboration with his librettist William Plomer, he composed three such works, sparsely scored for an ensemble consisting of flute, viola, horn, double bass, harp, percussion and organ. Their style owes much to the age-old Japanese Noh plays, as well as to Western plainsong, from which in each case the music grows. In the absence of a conductor, these operas demand a high degree of professionalism and mutual sympathy on the part of the performers, instrumentalists and vocalists alike, who are allowed considerable freedom in the interaction of their parts.

Curlew River received its first performance in Orford Church during the 1964 Aldeburgh Festival, after which it was taken on tour by the English Opera Group. Britten and Plomer took the traditional Japanese story of a mother's search for her lost son, but gave it a medieval monastic setting in the Fens. Both subsequent parables, *The Burning Fiery Furnace* and *The Prodigal Son*, are based on familiar Biblical stories.

In 1960 Britten met Mstislav Rostropovich. Here, to be sure, was an artist of generous personality and outstanding musicianship, possessing to the full those qualities that best fired Britten's imagination. The initial outcome of their association was the Cello Sonata of 1961, which was followed in the course of the next decade by the Cello Symphony, first performed in the Moscow Conservatory in March 1964, and three solo Suites. Peter Pears apart, probably his most fruitful collaboration was with the great Russian cellist.

During these years Britten paid tribute to the artistry of other admired friends. For Julian Bream he composed a *Nocturnal* for solo guitar, and for the baritone Dietrich Fischer-Dieskau, who had been a soloist in the first performance of the *War Requiem*, he wrote the song-cycle *Songs and Proverbs of William Blake*, which they performed together at the 1965 Aldeburgh Festival. Later that year, during a holiday in Armenia, he composed *The Poet's Echo*, a setting in Russian of six poems by Pushkin, which is dedicated to the soprano Galina Vishnevskaya and her cellist husband, Rostropovich, who took the less familiar role of piano accompanist.

There were, too, works written specifically for children's voices, including the *Missa Brevis* in D, *The Golden Vanity*, and the ballad *Children's Crusade* (the text by Brecht), which Britten composed for the boys of Wandsworth School Choir to mark the fiftieth anniversary of the Save the Children Fund. In terms of actual timbre, Britten's strong preference, which may be traced back to his hearing the Dutch boys in the première of his *Spring Symphony* at the 1949 Holland Festival, was for a rougher, harder-edged quality than is general among English cathedral choirs. In a lighter, though no less characteristic vein, he conceived the *Gemini Variations* (on a theme of Kodály) to show off the combined talents of the Jeney twins, two accomplished and extremely versatile young musicians whom he had met at a music club in Budapest.

Britten's return to full-length opera was prompted by a BBC commission for a work to be written specifically for the television medium. As his subject he chose *Owen Wingrave*, a short story by Henry James, which recounts the trials of a young man who, on grounds of conscience, rebels against his family's long military traditions and his own intended career. The theme, familiar from the far-off days of *Peter Grimes*, is that of the individual at odds with an unsympathetic society. To a degree, remarkable even for Britten, the parts were written with definite artists in mind. *Owen Wingrave* was transmitted by the BBC in May 1971 and the composer subsequently adapted it for stage performance.

Britten's final opera, *Death in Venice*, is an ingenious and highly imaginative adaptation of the novel by Thomas Mann. His librettist was again Myfanwy Piper, with whom he had collaborated on both the James-based operas. The choreography of the opera, in which there are important dance sequences, was devised by Sir Frederick Ashton. Britten, following Mann, explores in great depth the character of the central figure, the writer Aschenbach, his thoughts and obsessions; and incidentally creates for Peter Pears, to whom the work is dedicated, one of the most taxing roles in the whole repertoire. Of this opera, Britten said feelingly: 'Death in Venice is everything that Peter and I have stood for'. Its luminous, radiant, yet sparsely scored closing bars dissolve, as it feels, into infinity.

While he was still working on Death in Venice, Britten learned that he urgently needed heart surgery to replace a malfunctioning valve, but he was determined to postpone the operation until he had completed the score. The first performance of the opera, conducted by Steuart Bedford, took place at The Maltings in June 1973. The composer was convalescing at the time and unable to take any part. His illness, for the operation afforded no more than partial relief, greatly restricted the range of Britten's activities and, perhaps most poignantly, brought to an end his concerts with Peter Pears. An upshot was that Pears began to work extensively with the harpist Osian Ellis and Britten responded practically by composing a short series of works for them to perform in recital. For Osian Ellis, he had already written a Suite for solo harp, which was now followed by Canticle V, The Death of Saint Narcissus (to an early poem by T.S. Eliot), for tenor and harp, and A Birthday Hansel, his delightful Robert Burns song cycle. There were also some new folk-song arrangements for the duo.

Towards the end of his life Britten began to review some of his earlier compositions. The String Quartet of 1931, hitherto unpublished, was heard for the first time during the 1975 Aldeburgh Festival, and a revised version of the opera *Paul Bunyan* was broadcast in a concert performance by BBC radio early in 1976 and staged at The Maltings that summer. Britten found that such activity helped to restore his confidence and bring him to terms with composition again after his operation.

In addition to his new works for the Pears-Ellis duo, he was able to compose for orchestra during the winter of 1974-1975 a *Suite on English Folk Tunes*, which he dedicated to the memory of Percy Grainger, and *Sacred and Profane*, settings of eight medieval lyrics for unaccompanied voices.

To this group of small-scale works belong two of his very finest inspirations, the cantata *Phaedra* and his String Quartet No.3. For *Phaedra*, a dramatic cantata for mezzo-soprano and small orchestra, composed for Janet Baker, Britten selected four passages from Robert Lowell's verse translation of Racine's *Phèdre*. An absolute masterpiece, *Phaedra* is a work of extraordinary passion and feeling and contains a sense of an almost ecstatic acceptance of death; at its première the audience marvelled that such an outpouring of feeling was possible from the pen of a man himself facing the end. The quartet, his first composition for this medium for thirty years, was completed during a visit to Venice, a city that always stirred him, in November 1975. Its haunting finale (its subtitle *La Serenissima*) takes the form of a slow-moving passacaglia and draws on material from his last opera. The work ends, as it seems, on a questioning note. The textures are sparse and yet luminous. These remarkable late works – the opera, the cantata and the quartet – may be felt to breathe a spirit of renewal, perhaps reflecting a hard-won self-acceptance on the part of the composer.

Despite his disability, Britten continued to compose, although his working hours were of necessity limited. He faced growing infirmity with characteristic resolution and stoicism. In June 1976 he was created a Life Peer, the first composer to receive such an honour. That summer, for the young musicians of Suffolk, he wrote a short, high-spirited *Welcome Ode*, which was his last completed score. He died at home in Aldeburgh on 4 December 1976. Barely a fortnight later the Amadeus Quartet gave the first performance at The Maltings of the String Quartet No.3, which was at once recognised as one of his greatest achievements.

Certain threads run through the corpus of Britten's achievements: a sense of the cruelty of the world and the fragility of existence; a fierce sympathy for the outsider, the individual who cannot conform to society's expectations; and the corruption of innocence. Herein perhaps lies an element of his enduring appeal in a society that may seem increasingly fractured.

That the artist must remain accessible to his audience was one of Britten's most deeply-held convictions. For children especially he wrote with unique insight and sympathy, while the encouragement he gave to amateur music-making is indicative of the special concern he felt for the wellbeing of English musical life in the broadest sense. His work as an educator found fulfilment in the opening at The Maltings of a School for Advanced Musical Studies, intended to help young musicians, specifically singers and string players, at the start of their professional careers. As an intensely practical musician and a composer of genius, Benjamin Britten speaks directly to us.

2.

The composer: personality, influences, friends and circle

Any view of the crucial formative influences on the young Britten must start with the composer Frank Bridge (1879-1941) and the poet W.H. Auden (1907-1973).

With Bridge, a much older man, there was a remarkable personal affinity grounded in common ideals and interests: pacifism, left-wing politics, tennis (Britten was always a fiercely competitive player!). Bridge grasped at once the boy's immense promise. The 'mammoth' (Britten's word) private lessons in composition in London and at Bridge's home at Friston, Sussex began in 1927; they were rigorous and utterly professional. Bridge set exacting standards; no sloppiness was tolerated. To the end of his life Britten would ask himself if his own work had lived up to the standards that Bridge had set. Above all, perhaps, he learnt the importance of finding himself and expressing with total clarity what he had in mind; and that good technique was a prerequisite.

Britten met the poet Wystan Auden, almost seven years his senior, in July 1935 when they were collaborating on short documentary films – *Coal Face* and *Night Mail* – at the GPO Film Unit. Both men had benefited from attending a liberal and progressive public school, Gresham's at Holt; the officers' training corps was not compulsory and the principle of conscientious objection respected. Their major collaborations, notably *Our Hunting Fathers* (regarded by Britten as his 'real' Opus 1), its backdrop the deeply troubled 1930s in Europe, were early ones. Auden, also a man of the left, was knowledgeable, authoritative, and possessor of a didactic manner; he characteristically felt a certain compulsion to advise his friends about their mode of life. 'Benjy', as Auden called him, was far less sure of himself and minded to keep his intimate life to himself; he felt an 'appalling inferiority complex' in the company of his domineering friend. Later in life, Auden adopted the view that art was powerless to change the world, a position which Britten never quite came to share. If their relationship was at times uneasy, Britten was – as Peter Pears remarked – 'full of admiration and gratitude for the earlier years'. For his part, Auden always expressed his admiration for his old friend's music.

Peter Pears (1910-1986), the tenor, was Britten's life companion and creative muse. It was Pears who inspired the tremendous series of song cycles and operatic roles, conceived mainly with his highly-distinctive voice in mind, and for which Britten is most remembered. Like the composer, Pears attended a 'liberal' public school, Lancing College ('a very heaven'). He then proceeded to Oxford but left without taking a degree. His background was upper middle-class, his forebears mainly clergy and military officers.

Pears and Britten first met in 1934 when Pears was a member of the BBC Singers. Their recitals, from 1937 onwards, became among the most keenly anticipated events in the musical calendar, both in England and much further afield. Pears was already a man of wide culture and with a remarkable sensitivity to the potential of setting texts to music. Whilst not everyone responded to his highly-distinctive tenor, the intelligence that informed his singing was universally acknowledged. Composer and muse shared the same fundamentally high-principled liberal outlook. There were differences, though. Pears, a professional singer in great demand, enjoyed the bright lights of London, of the city, whereas Britten was happiest and most fulfilled only when composing at home in Suffolk. He was unhappy that Pears, with his nomadic lifestyle, was so often away. Steuart Bedford, much later Britten's trusted surrogate conductor following his illness, observed that Britten was much more emotionally buttoned-up than Pears. The singer, too, had a certain 'schoolmasterly' bearing and was a touch forbidding – quite unlike Britten. Courteous and agreeable in manner, he was seen by many as finally unknowable.

It was in 1939 in America that, in Pears's words, they realised that they were 'in love with each other'. In Grand

Rapids they entered into a 'pledge', which brought the composer a new happiness and freedom. They did not flaunt their lifestyle, however, and Pears later remarked that there was 'a streak of the puritan' in his lover. In a film made after Britten's death, the singer spoke with frankness and emotion about a relationship that was 'passionately devoted and close'.

It was Pears who suggested in 1947 that they should have their own festival at home in Aldeburgh; the first festival was held from 5 to 13 June 1948. Britten and Pears, greatly helped by Imogen Holst (the composer Gustav Holst's daughter, and utterly devoted to Britten and the festival), were totally proficient in the running of the artistic side; a lively exchange of ideas would always inform the planning. When, later in life, Britten became too ill to play, he encouraged Pears to perform – and to memorable effect – with the pianist Murray Perahia, then near the start of his career, and the harpist Osian Ellis. It may truly be said that his final opera *Death in Venice* – the central role of Aschenbach, conceived for Pears's voice and certainly the most demanding of his career – is the supreme testimony of his love for his singer.

Without his unique bond with Pears, Britten's creative life might – for better or for worse – have followed a quite different trajectory. One may regret, for example, the absence of a big orchestral piece, a successor to *Sinfonia da Requiem*, or a major work for solo piano. So much for what might have been; finally, though, we must be grateful for the riches we have.

With his slightly older contemporary Michael Tippett (1905-1998), Britten had a long-standing friendship, grounded in deep mutual respect and admiration. Britten and Tippett: the names often associated in the public mind – perhaps also reinforced by the then not uncommon sight of vehicles bearing the inscription 'Tibbett and Britten' – occupied a position of special eminence amongst living English composers since the death of Ralph Vaughan Williams in 1958. Certainly they had much in common: both were gay, of socialist conviction and committed to pacifism. Temperamentally, though, the differences were no less striking: Tippett was not in the least 'buttoned-up' emotionally, and the moralistic, conventionally respectable strand in Britten's character was not something he shared. His spontaneous reaction to the double-entendre – 'clear the decks of seamen' – in a draft of the *Billy Budd* libretto with its all-male cast is revealing. Tippett, relishing the stage direction, was reduced to gales of laughter; Britten and Pears, apparently, were not amused.

On a personal level, Britten was moved by Tippett's imprisonment at Wormwood Scrubs for refusing to accept the terms of his exemption from military service. Tippett's cantata *Boyhood's End* (1943) was the first work by another composer that the Britten-Pears partnership inspired. It is clear that Britten's admiration for Tippett was genuine; always self-critical, he sometimes asked himself if his own music, for all its technical assurance, lacked his friend's 'depth'.

Amongst contemporary composers, Britten probably felt closest to the Russian Dmitri Shostakovich, with whom a deep and genuine friendship developed, initially through the agency of the great cellist Rostropovich. Britten dedicated his church parable *The Prodigal Son* (1968) to Shostakovich, and the Russian returned the compliment a year later with his Fourteenth Symphony, its topic the mortality of humankind. Both men were acutely aware of the darkness of the world, its misery and sadness, of man's inhumanity to man; both shared a deep compassion for the human condition; both had a passion to communicate. With Britten there also existed a strong feeling for redemption. Even as early as 1936, Britten had been hugely impressed by a concert performance of Shostakovich's opera *Lady Macbeth of the Mtsensk District*, a work which had incited Stalin's fury. According to Rostropovich, Shostakovich thought Britten's *War Requiem* the greatest work of the twentieth century. Shostakovich visited Aldeburgh only once, in 1972, and spent time at Britten's home, the Red House, while the composer was working on *Death in Venice*; the incomplete composition sketch enthralled him.

Britten also fell under the spell of Mahler at an early stage, well before the composer's renaissance in the 1960s. Britten's enthusiasm was aroused by a performance of Mahler's Fourth Symphony at a Promenade Concert at Queen's Hall in 1930; he singled out his orchestration, 'wonderful ear for sound' and 'great sense of form'. In 1937, on hearing a performance of *Das Lied von der Erde*, he spoke of 'basking' in the 'Heavenly light' of the work's final chord: 'it is worth having lived to do that'. Britten's great desire to study in Vienna with Mahler's admirer Alban Berg was thwarted, probably blocked by the authorities at the Royal College.

Britten had a very clear conception of how his own compositions should be performed; his scores were very clearly marked. If he felt that professional musicians, however eminent, and especially singers, were 'interpreting' his music in ways alien to its spirit, or a performance was inadequate, he would become frustrated, depressed, even angry. For this reason Britten often preferred the sincerity of amateur performances that had the right intent. The bond he formed with Steuart Bedford was especially significant. Here was someone who instinctively understood and had the skills to realise in performance the intention behind the notes on the page. Britten also took part in amateur music-making in Aldeburgh, sometimes playing viola on the instrument bequeathed to him by Frank Bridge. His deep desire to be 'useful' included service to the local community. The miniature opera *Noye's Fludde* was envisaged very much as a true community piece for young and old, professional and amateur, skilled and unskilled. At the time it gave enormous impetus to children's and amateur music-making.

Possibly more than any other composer in musical history, Britten was inspired by the musicianship of particular singers and instrumentalists. For him the personal was always uppermost. Underpinning this was a complete understanding of the technical possibilities and challenges of every instrument for which he was writing. Early in his career the incomparable horn player Dennis Brain, tragically killed in a car crash at the age of 36, was an inspirational figure – along with Peter Pears – in the creation of the *Serenade* for tenor, horn and strings (1943). Much later the remarkable Rostropovich inspired a whole series of significant compositions for his instrument. Composer and performer would communicate in a form of German called 'Aldeburgh Deutsch'!

The guitarist and lutenist Julian Bream, who regularly accompanied Pears, was another close friend and admirer of the composer, and an Aldeburgh regular – the *Nocturnal after John Dowland* for guitar was written for him. Finding himself unaccountably 'dropped' from the festival roster of artists, and unable to discover the reason, he approached his friend the composer William Walton. Britten's response, communicated by Pears to Walton, was frustratingly opaque and left Bream none the wiser: 'My dear, it's his Dowland. It's slipping.' (This answer became a source of great amusement to the two friends whenever they met.) And Bream, who never stopped performing with Pears, was soon back!

According to Eric Crozier, librettist and opera producer, Britten himself spoke ruefully of his 'corpses', artists and friends who were dropped from the festival without explanation. He was uncommonly thin-skinned. The impression that emerges is of a 'court' atmosphere with a close circle of associates protecting the insecure, vulnerable composer from the outside world, safeguarding his privacy. There was a shell round him. Yet in a friendly circle he could be fun to be with, an amusing and witty conversationalist. He was always deeply sensitive to criticism, especially when he considered it to be ill-informed and therefore unjust.

This 'basic insecurity' is mentioned by Stephen Reiss in conversation with Alan Blyth (*Remembering Britten*, 1981). Reiss, supremely competent and highly respected, was general manager of the Aldeburgh Festival until his 'fall from grace' in 1971, leading to an acute sense of betrayal. It was he above all who rescued the festival following the disastrous Maltings fire in 1969. He and his wife and Britten and Pears had been very close. 'You were either in or out'. Most interestingly, Reiss believed that Britten's hypersensitivity about people talking behind his back arose from a basic insecurity, the consequence of his having adopted 'an unconventional life-style in the context of an exceptionally conventional upbringing and fundamental adherence to traditional moral values.'

Leonard Bernstein, who conducted the American première of *Peter Grimes* at Tanglewood (the Boston Symphony's summer home), found Britten at the same time 'diffident' and unyielding in his opinions. He described him in the film *A Time There Was*, as 'a man at odds with the world … There are gears that are grinding and not quite meshing …'

Genius is always prone to excite jealousy. There were a few barbed comments about 'the Mozart of Aldeburgh'. But composition, as Britten understood no less than Mozart, involves, above all, solid hard work and false starts. Britten, being the person he was – and with the barely sustainable triple role of composer, performing artist and festival director – was in need of this protective layer of support. There was also the burden of expectation. This was a time – now gone forever – when, as this writer recalls, new works by the likes of Britten, Tippett and Shostakovich were keenly anticipated, even widely reported events.

The rifts notwithstanding, one is finally struck by the level of goodwill and genuine affection that Britten inspired. Michael Tippett's obituary notice expressed it thus: '… I think that all of us who were close to Ben had for him something dangerously near to love …'. For all his prodigious musical gifts – perhaps never seen in this country before – he was a man who loved Aldeburgh, his walks along its shingly beach, his county of Suffolk, its historic churches, his dachshunds and (rather touchingly) the plain cooking – his preference was for 'nursery food', such as milk pudding and spotted dick – served up by his and Pears's housekeeper Miss

Hudson. His celebrated Alvis and, earlier, a Rolls Royce were among his few concessions to personal luxury.

By common consent Britten was 'wonderful' to work for. But at times he could be tetchy, ruthless and unforgiving. The distinguished Welsh tenor Robert Tear, whose feelings about the man and his music were ambivalent, recalled how Britten once 'astonished' him by accusing him of using his music 'as a vocal exercise'. However, the composer could also be 'so wonderfully charming'. The truth probably is that Britten was always bound to have in his head Pears's voice, technique and interpretation. The Canadian tenor Jon Vickers's highly regarded interpretation of Peter Grimes also met with a strongly adverse reaction from the composer.

The singer Janet Baker, speaking to Alan Blyth, described Britten as 'a very attractive personality who drew people to him like moths to a flame.' Whilst there was genuine affection on both sides, Baker prudently decided not to get too close to the sun for fear of being burnt. Other colleagues also recognised the danger of getting involved too closely.

Colin Graham was one of Britten's longest-standing collaborators, both as producer and designer, then as one of the directors of the Aldeburgh Festival. He directed all of the composer's world premières after 1954. Graham had the deepest admiration for Britten, with whom he had a close friendship, describing him as 'a kind of surrogate father'. He recalled Britten's extraordinary depth of knowledge about the whole repertoire. Their artistic relationship was a truly collaborative one, and Graham always found the composer open to his ideas. He recognised that, for Britten, nothing less than total commitment and loyalty were expected: 'Inclinations in other directions were not always smiled on'.

Britten set the highest standards both for himself and others. A lack of professionalism would anger him. This had a most unfortunate outcome in a misunderstanding involving the keyboard player Viola Tunnard, a devoted member of Britten's circle during the 1960s. She was experiencing the onset of Motor Neurone Disease and her playing was suffering. Britten, unaware of this, only knew that she was failing to deliver. He became frustrated and angry. It is said that Britten subsequently was in agony when, discovering her condition, he realised that he had been very unkind to her.

Britten's charm was often spoken of as a defining characteristic. Joan Cross, the soprano and opera director, who created the role of Ellen Orford in *Peter Grimes*, knew Britten well: 'a man of great charm and a glorious sense of humour, given to occasional and sudden bursts of fury (which he often regretted later) and of course total dedication.' She believed that Britten needed few close friends; his relationship with Pears 'satisfied his needs musically, intellectually and emotionally.' Leonard Bernstein put it this way: 'Peter Pears … represented for him all relationships put together … which … made it difficult for him to have other deep friendships.'

The composer developed a special connection with the remarkable 200-strong Wandsworth School Boys' Choir under its inspirational director, Russell Burgess. 'My favourite choir at my favourite school'. He responded to the earthy, unsophisticated quality of the choir's singing (very different from the 'cathedral sound'). The boys would have the run of the Red House, the swimming pool and tennis court when visiting Aldeburgh to perform. Britten loved the company of young people: their freshness, their vitality, their idealism. He took a fatherly interest in boys, often the sons of friends, who came to stay at the Red House. On occasion he would give members of the Aldeburgh Youth Club his foreign stamps, from the hundreds of letters he received from abroad.

Britten's silence on his homosexuality is suggestive of a profound unwillingness to be regarded as any kind of standard-bearer for 'gay liberation'. With his persecution complex, he knew well enough that this unconventional side of his character made him a potential target. His connections with some of the highest in the land can only have brought him, therefore, a degree of stress.

Britten liked people to behave 'properly' and take their morals seriously. As Peter Pears put it, he believed that decent behaviour and manners were part of a fine life. Coming from a conventional middle-class background, he had viewed with distaste the boasted promiscuity and bohemianism of Auden and some of his circle. He found it hard to forgive people who offended his own code of behaviour. Some found it hard to accept this fiercely moralistic streak in the composer. When, for example, his close friend the Earl of Harewood's first marriage foundered, Britten, taking his wife's side, chose not to see him for three years.

The composer's acceptance, in the last year of his life, of a Life Peerage caused surprise in some quarters. However Britten – unlike those 'liberals' of today who continue to accept redundant imperial honours – enjoyed a personal friendship both with his sovereign and her mother, patron of the Aldeburgh Festival, for whose 75th birthday *A Birthday Hansel* was written.

So we have here a composer of genius – of that there can be no doubt – who lived absolutely for his art. A strong work ethic was combined with an overwhelming desire 'to be useful and to the living'. Britten was a man of great charm and fine ideals, whose behaviour could also present challenges to his close collaborators. It is recorded that he performed many acts of personal kindness to a wide range of people. Imogen Holst noted in her diary that Ben 'had a very strong feeling that people died at the right moment'. When Britten could no longer compose, he died.

3.

The composer as performer

B enjamin Britten was universally acknowledged to have a pre-eminence as an accompanist to singers and instrumentalists. Only Gerald Moore, self-effacingly describing Britten as 'the world's greatest accompanist', was widely regarded as his peer in this specialist genre. Even Stravinsky, who followed Britten's compositional career more closely than he cared to admit, could not withhold recognition of his special gift. More than that, Britten was widely felt to be a great conductor, both of his own and other composers' music, when standing in front of an orchestra and large choral forces.

When Britten sat at the keyboard, listeners would speak of a sense of 're-creation' – to be absolutely distinguished from 'interpretation'! – of a composer's musical landscape. Such was his degree of empathy with the composer's inner vision, with the notes on the page. Whilst Britten was accomplished enough to be the soloist at the first performance of his technically demanding Piano Concerto (1938), he was not himself a 'concert pianist' in the accepted sense. This is highly significant. For Britten was first and foremost a composer, possessing – in his case to an almost uncanny degree – a composer's insight and empathy.

Several of Britten's colleagues identified the qualities that made working with him so infinitely rewarding: a warmth and generosity of phrasing, allowing the music to emerge with a sense of freshness and inevitability; a feeling for line and quality of tone and ensemble; a meticulous attention to detail and the composer's expressed wishes; and a sense of pulse. His performances, for all his scrupulous regard for the printed score, never feel unyielding or inflexible. Janet Baker recalled the clarity of his beat and the sureness of his tempi; performers felt a rare sense of security. Robert Tear spoke of the 'inner passion' that infused all his music-making. For the violinist Emanuel Hurwitz, leader of the English Chamber Orchestra, he was 'a quite wonderful conductor in the greatest sense of the word. He made the orchestra feel they wanted to play for him'.

Britten, as has been noted, did not appreciate artists 'interpreting' his music. The markings in the score were all sufficient. A striking contrast may be tentatively suggested here with Johannes Brahms, a composer for whose music, a few early works excepted, Britten felt a strong antipathy; he found it lacking spontaneity, freshness and to be thickly scored. Interestingly, the German master is known to have allowed a considerable amount of latitude in performances, including his own, to the extent that even his great friend Clara Schumann was discomforted on occasion. This freedom also extended, controversially, to the playing of marked repeats. Britten, by contrast, in keeping with current performance practice, was punctilious about repeats being observed. It is remarkable that his studio recording with the English Chamber Orchestra of Mozart's Symphony No. 40 in G minor, all repeats taken, lasts close on 38 minutes. His 1966 performance in Blythburgh Church of Symphony No. 41 in C ('Jupiter') with the same forces, gloriously warm and fresh, and with dynamics carefully differentiated, is of similar duration.

Britten's view of the place of recordings – expressed in his speech 'On Receiving the first Aspen Award' (1963) for services to the humanities – was deeply ambivalent. The electronic reproduction of music was a surrogate for the true musical experience. Britten valued it 'as a means of education and study, or as an evoker of memories'. Yet the recordings he made, often under the auspices of the brilliant producer John Culshaw, were always informed by the surest of musical instincts.

It is Britten's live performances that, generally speaking, most movingly enshrine the spirit of the man; a frisson of nervous tension lends a spontaneity that most often eludes all the craft of the recording studio. But they were preceded by agonies of nervous apprehension and often physical sickness. This was more especially true of recitals – brandy might be called for. Britten was always more relaxed when performing in Aldeburgh, less comfortable in London. For him music was, above all, a living art. He spoke movingly of the 'holy triangle': the unique relationship between composer, performer and audience.

Two surviving live Mozart concerto performances (K414 and K459), Britten directing from the keyboard, respectively, the Aldeburgh Festival Orchestra and The English Opera Group Chamber Orchestra, display those characteristic Britten traits: freshness of discovery, spontaneity, clarity of articulation. One commentator at the time remarked: '… He plays a Mozart concerto … not merely as if he had written it, but as if he had written it last night'. Britten relished making music with friends, amongst whom may also be numbered some of the finest British orchestral musicians of his time (as was true also of that other 'outsider', Edward Elgar). They repaid him with absolute trust and confidence.

Britten's relationships with two great Russian musicians, the pianist Sviatoslav Richter and the cellist Mstislav Rostropovich, are especially worthy of celebration. For the latter's instrument a highly significant body of new work was composed. Here a parallel may perhaps be drawn – albeit a cautionary one, given Britten's sensitivities! – with the artistry of another instrumentalist, Richard Mühlfeld, clarinettist in the Meiningen Orchestra, whose artistry inspired Brahms to leave retirement.

Britten's connection with Richter – regarded by Prokofiev (and subsequently Britten too) as the best pianist in the world – was particularly strong. The two men, introduced by Rostropovich in 1961, collaborated memorably in Mozart's last Piano Concerto (K595 in B flat) in Blythburgh's unique ambience during the 1965 festival. (Britten's celebrated studio recording with his long-standing friend Clifford Curzon and the English Chamber Orchestra followed five years later.)

In 1967 Britten and Richter performed the great E flat Concerto (K482) at the Snape Maltings; for this occasion Britten, at Richter's request, wrote cadenzas (Mozart left none of his own), and chose to deploy the full sonority of the modern concert grand in some unashamedly virtuoso passage-work.

Richter came to love Aldeburgh, which he visited for several years running during the 1960s. He was known to perform unscheduled concerts during the festival. He considered Britten 'a true friend' and 'so sympathetic'; his conducting was 'magnificent'. Together they performed works for two pianos and piano duets by Mozart, Schubert and also Debussy (*En blanc et noir*). The Mozart performances (Sonatas in D K448 and in C K521) possess a wonderful unanimity; each man gives his personality full rein but never to the detriment of the other's; together, they show a scrupulous regard for the composer's text. They also shared another deep conviction: all the indicated repeats must be observed!

Their Schubert playing possesses the same spirit of intimacy and communion. On 22 June 1965 the audience in Aldeburgh's Jubilee Hall witnessed a truly great occasion, thankfully preserved for posterity. Britten and Richter performed two late Schubert masterworks, the F minor Fantasy and the Grand Duo in C major, music-making of extraordinary communicative power that (in this writer's opinion) leaves all other performances in the shade. Britten's connection with Schubert was unique, deeply personal and lifelong. He loved his gift of melody, the depth of the music's flow; the bond was almost spiritual. In the case of Beethoven, Schubert's revered and almost unapproachable hero, Britten's early admiration gave way to a deep ambivalence; in contrast to Schubert's spontaneity, he came to think of Beethoven's music as too 'intellectual'.

At the 1961 festival Rostropovich and Britten collaborated in a remarkably diverse range of repertoire, including Schubert's Arpeggione Sonata, Debussy's Cello Sonata, and Schumann's Five Pieces in Folk Style. They also performed together Britten's friend Shostakovich's Cello Sonata and Janáček's little-known *Fairy Tale* for cello and piano; Britten's mentor Frank Bridge's Phantasy Quartet (performed with members of the Amadeus Quartet) was also not overlooked. Rostropovich, with the composer at the piano, gave the first performance of Britten's Cello Sonata also in 1961. The cellist, ebullient and outgoing, and Britten, introverted and somewhat repressed, complemented each other magnificently.

The Amadeus Quartet, for whom the valedictory String Quartet No. 3 was written, were long-standing friends of the composer. In 1967 the duo of Norbert Brainin (violin) and Peter Schidlof (viola) played Mozart's sublime Sinfonia Concertante – a 'corker' of a work Britten called it – under his direction at the Queen Elizabeth Hall. Britten was a supremely accomplished pianist in any chamber music combination, whatever the repertoire. As early as 1953 Amadeus members had joined with him in a performance of Mozart's Piano Quartet in E flat (K493). Britten's 1971 performance with his string-playing colleagues, Kenneth Sillito, Cecil Aronowitz and Kenneth Heath, of the Piano Quartet in G minor (K478) may be taken as an outstanding example of his art. Here the piano 'sings' as eloquently as any string instrument; scrupulous attention is paid to Mozart's markings. There is a wonderful sense of dialogue between the artists.

Aldeburgh, then, was a gathering of friends making music together and finding inspiration. The geographical spread of musicians participating was remarkable, including (as we have seen) those from the Soviet bloc. Britten, Pears and Imogen Holst (also an artistic director of the festival) always sought to plan events of more general interest to local people as well as the wider arts community.

Among Britten's live orchestral performances, his 1961 performance of Mahler's Fourth Symphony with the London Symphony Orchestra at Orford Church has special interest. Britten had discovered 'my precious Mahler 4th', 'that great work' he called it, as early as the 1930s and well before Mahler acquired anything akin to a cult following in this country. The first movement, taken at an uncommonly fast pace, possesses a unique freshness and sense of exhilaration. As always, Britten shows scrupulous concern for the detailed dynamics. His admiring description of Mahler's music as 'clean and transparent' is very much in keeping with his own performance practice.

Recordings that Britten made of music by his great predecessors Edward Elgar and Ralph Vaughan Williams possess their own rewards. With the music of Elgar, Britten had an unquiet relationship, though he developed a feeling for this composer later in life. His studio performance of *Introduction and Allegro* for strings possesses tremendous fire and urgency; and his recording of *The Dream of Gerontius*, urgent and unsentimental, is widely esteemed. His 1945 recording of Vaughan Williams' *On Wenlock Edge* with the Zorian Quartet, with Britten at the piano and Pears as tenor, shows an instinctive ability to identify with the vision of a composer inhabiting a quite different musical landscape from his own. As a very young man seeking to find himself, and with Frank Bridge as his mentor, he had spoken critically of RVW's 'amateurishness', though in a letter of condolence to the composer's widow Ursula he referred to him as 'a tremendous figure to me'.

Britten (and Michael Tippett also) acknowledged a particular debt to the example of Henry Purcell, England's great Baroque composer, who had a profound influence on Britten's word-setting. His interest in Purcell, whose music he edited extensively, burgeoned in the early 1940s when he made his first keyboard realisations of his songs. Britten was insistent that it was chiefly through Purcell's example that he came to understand the effective setting of English poetry. He recorded his own editions of the G minor Chacony, the opera *Dido and Aeneas* and the masque *The Fairy Queen*.

Of the music of J.S. Bach, Britten made just two commercial recordings: the *Brandenburg Concertos* in 1968, full of vitality, and the *St John Passion* in 1971, with Pears as Evangelist. The concertos gave his friends in the English Chamber Orchestra – very much Aldeburgh's 'house' orchestra in the 1960s – abundant scope to display their remarkable talents. (The Busch Chamber Players' legendary recordings from the 1930s remain forever *hors concours* in this repertoire.)

The astonishingly wide range of music that, as a performer, Britten presented to Aldeburgh audiences is, even now perhaps, not fully appreciated. Particular mention may be made here of the extraordinary Percy Grainger, whose uniquely original voice found in Britten an unstinting advocate. Neither did the festival neglect composers with whose music Britten might seem to be less in sympathy – it is notable that he played Brahms' piano duets with Claudio Arrau.

Nonetheless, it is probably his and Pears's recitals of Schubert's great song cycles and other lieder that resonate most strongly in the public mind. In *Winterreise* Britten seems almost to be re-creating each song at the very moment of performance; one is genuinely brought to share the poet's heartbreak on realising that any happiness is merely a dream. Every note, as Britten understood it, had a vital relationship to the text. Cognoscenti spoke of the beauty of the piano sound, the sense of colour, the sense of timing and Britten's remarkable ability to make the piano speak as eloquently as the voice. Underpinning all was his empathy with his partner, an extraordinary shared vision and sympathy; one might speak of their recitals as a musical mirror of their personal intimacy. Often, to lighten the mood, these recitals would end with a selection of Britten's folk-song arrangements.

Britten's genius as a performing artist may be felt to lie in his unerring ability to understand a composer's vision and to communicate its essence to his colleagues and audiences. From his early days he was deeply suspicious of the persona of the 'great conductor', who might be presenting an 'interpretation' at variance with a work's true nature, as he understood it. His friend Dietrich Fischer-Dieskau, the

German baritone, commented: 'Unlike so many conductors, he had no mannerisms at all … No one ever caught him playing a role.' Robert Tear, for all his reservations about the man, was unequivocal: Britten was without doubt the greatest musician and conductor he had ever known.

Appendix

Letter to the author from Sir Peter Pears CBE*

THE RED HOUSE, ALDEBURGH-ON-SEA, SUFFOLK, IP15 5PZ.

march 1st

Dear Timothy Gilbert.

This is a very late answer to your letter of February 1st. As you probably know I have been disabled through a stroke.

Thank you for sending me your essay which I have enjoyed reading. It is straightforward, clear, & accurate, qualities which its subject would have much appreciated – I am enclosing the cards of Ben's window here, which you will not have seen yet, I fancy –

with all good wishes

yours sincerely

from SIR PETER PEARS CBE

Peter Pears

* Sir Peter's comments relate only to an early version of the 'Biographical outline' section of the text.

By the same author

Reflections: Eight King Henrys
ISBN: 978-1-85858-774-5, £7.95

Available at: www.brewinbooks.com

The final resting place of Benjamin Britten and Peter Pears at St Peter and St Paul's Church, Aldeburgh (author's photograph).